MY WORLD OF SCIENCE

# Forces and Motion

### Revised and Updated

Angela Royston

Heinemann
LIBRARY

# H www.heinemann.co.uk/library
Visit our website to find out more information about Heinemann Library books.

To order:
☎ Phone 44 (0) 1865 888066
🖹 Send a fax to 44 (0) 1865 314091
🖳 Visit the Heinemann Bookshop at www.heinemann.co.uk/library to browse our catalogue and order online.

First published in Great Britain by Heinemann Library, Halley Court, Jordan Hill, Oxford OX2 8EJ, part of Pearson Education. Heinemann is a registered trademark of Pearson Education Ltd.

Editorial: Diyan Leake
Design: Joanna Hinton-Malivoire
Picture research: Melissa Allison and Mica Brancic
Production: Alison Parsons

Originated by Chroma Graphics (Overseas) Pte Ltd
Printed and bound in China by South China Printing Co. Ltd

ISBN 978 0 431 13765 0 (hardback)
12 11 10 09 08
10 9 8 7 6 5 4 3 2 1

ISBN 978 0 431 13788 9 (paperback)
12 11 10 09 08
10 9 8 7 6 5 4 3 2 1

## British Library Cataloguing in Publication Data
Royston, Angela
Forces and motion. – New ed. - (My world of science)
   1. Motion – Juvenile literature  2. Force and energy – Juvenile literature
   I. Title
   531.1'13

## Acknowledgements
The publishers would like to thank the following for permission to reproduce photographs: © Alamy/Arco Images p. 19; © Bubbles p. 26 (Frans Rombout); © Corbis pp. 8, 11, 16, 20 (Henrykk Trigg), 28, 29; © Powerstock Zefa p. 10; © Robert Harding p. 5; © Science Photo Library pp. 6 (Dr Marley Read), 7 (Maximillian Stock); © Stone pp. 8, 12, 13; © Trevor Clifford pp. 14, 15, 17, 18, 21, 22, 23, 24, 25; © Trip pp. 4 (H. Rogers), 27 (P. Aikman), .

Cover photograph reproduced with permission of © Getty Images/Wild Pics.

The publishers would like to thank Jon Bliss for his assistance in the preparation of this book.

Every effort has been made to contact copyright holders of any material reproduced in this book. Any omissions will be rectified in subsequent printings if notice is given to the publishers.

# Contents

Any words appearing in the text in bold, **like this**, are explained in the glossary.

# What is a force?

A force makes things move. These people are moving a piano. One man is pushing it. The other man is pulling it.

Pulls and pushes are forces. This rider is pushing down on the pedals to make the bicycle wheels move forward.

# Machines and forces

This bulldozer is pushing earth and trees out of the way. Machines have **engines** that make the force to move heavy loads.

jib

cable

This crane is lifting a heavy load. The engine makes a force that moves the jib. The jib pulls up the cable and the cable pulls up the load.

# Natural forces

Wind and moving water are powerful **natural** forces. Wind is air that is moving. It can bend trees and push leaves through the air.

Moving water also pushes things. This boat is floating down a river. The moving water is a force that pushes the boat.

# Moving your body

We use our **muscles** to make our body move. Muscles can push and pull the different parts of our body.

This climber is pushing and pulling herself up a steep rock.

You can move in many different ways.
This woman is swimming. The muscles
in her arms, legs, and feet make a force
that moves her through the water.

# Stopping

Forces can also be used to stop something moving. This dog wants to move forwards. But its owner is pulling it backwards, to stop it.

Pushing or pulling against something that is moving can slow it down or stop it. The players in yellow are pulling the player in white. They are trying to stop him.

# Changing shape

Forces can be used to make some things change shape. It is easy to pull and push soft play dough into many different shapes.

This boy is squashing an empty carton. This will make the carton flatter and smaller, so it will take up less space in the dustbin.

Squashing an empty carton pushes the air out of it.

# Changing direction

Forces can make something change direction. This tennis player is pushing his racquet against the ball. The ball changes direction and goes back across the net.

Forces can also make something turn in a circle. You have to twist the top of a jar one way to get it off. You twist it the other way to put the top on.

# Moving further

The harder you push something, the faster it moves. This girl is pushing a toy train across the floor. If she gives it a big push, it will go faster and further.

This **athlete** is working hard to jump as far as he can. He pushes his feet down and backwards on the ground to move himself up and forwards.

# Slopes

A **slope** can change how fast something moves. This person is skiing down a slope. The **steeper** the slope, the faster the skier will move.

This woman is pushing her wheelbarrow up a slope. Pushing up a slope is harder than pushing on flat ground.

# Friction

**Friction** is a force that slows things down. This boy is pushing the toy digger and then letting go. The digger moves quickly at first, then it slows down and stops.

The digger slows down because its wheels rub against the ground. The rubbing is called friction. **Rough** wheels cause more friction than smooth wheels.

# Testing friction

This boy is using balls and a **ramp** to test which kind of floor has the most **friction** – carpet or wood. He measures how far the ball rolls.

carpet

ramp

The carpet is **rough** and the wood is smooth. Does the ball roll further on the carpet or on the wood? (Answer on page 31.)

wood

# Using friction

People can use **friction** to slow themselves down. When children push their arms and feet against the sides of a slide, the friction will slow them down.

This boy's hands will get warm as he pushes, because friction creates heat.

Bicycle brakes use friction to slow down. When you pull the brake handle, two rubber blocks grip against the wheel. This stops the wheel from moving so freely.

brake block

# More and less friction

The **soles** of your shoes are **rough**. They create **friction** between your feet and the ground. Friction stops you slipping when you move your feet.

Some soles have a pattern to create even more friction.

The less friction there is, the more you slide. Snow is very smooth, so there is very little friction. Skiers slide fast across the slippery snow.

# Glossary

**athlete**  person who takes part in a running, jumping, or throwing sport

**engine**  something that uses electricity or fuel, such as petrol or diesel, to make a machine move

**friction**  rubbing between one object and another that slows movement down

**muscle**  part of your body that helps you move

**natural**  something made by nature, not by people or machines

**ramp**  something used to make a slope

**rough**  bumpy or uneven

**slope**  surface that goes upward or downward

**sole**  bottom of a shoe

**steep**  when a slope goes up or down very sharply

# Answer

**Page 25 –** The ball has rolled further on wood than on carpet, showing that there is less friction between the ball and the wood.

# More books to read

*Amazing Science: Forces and Movement,* Sally Hewitt (Hodder Wayland, 2006)

*Science in Your Life – Forces: The ups and downs,* Wendy Sadler (Raintree, 2005)

*Start-up Science: Forces and Movement,* Claire Llewellyn (Evans, 2004)

# Index